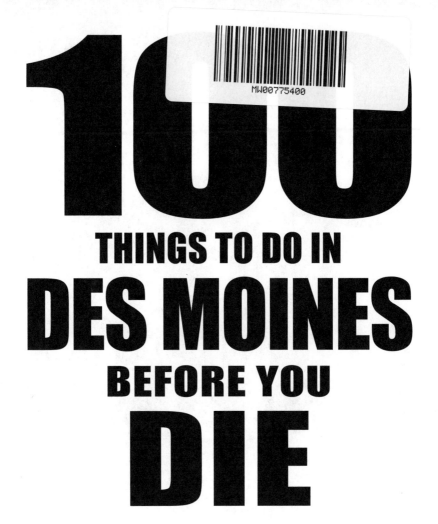

100
THINGS TO DO IN
DES MOINES
BEFORE YOU
DIE

Pappajohn Sculpture Park

100

THINGS TO DO IN
DES MOINES
BEFORE YOU
DIE

• •

ERIN HUIATT

REEDY PRESS

Library of Congress Control Number: 2023938759

ISBN: 9781681064581

Design by Jill Halpin

All images by the author unless otherwise noted.

Printed in the United States of America
23 24 25 26 27   5 4 3 2 1

DEDICATION

This book is dedicated to my father, Tony Epping. Without his love, sacrifice, and support, I would not be where I am today.

CONTENTS

● ●

Music and Entertainment

• •

• •

● ●

Culture and History

• •

Winterset Cidery

PREFACE

Des Moines has been a part of my life for over 25 years. Never in my wildest dreams did I think I would be sharing my love for this city and all of the amazing things to do. Growing up, the conversation among friends was always about getting out of Des Moines. Not me. I have stayed and it has been fun watching Des Moines blossom over the years. Today, many people who grew up here and went away now call this capital city home.

What brings them back? The people and the small-town feel with a big-city vibe.

Over the years, thousands of travelers have passed by our city without stopping. Not anymore! Des Moines is no longer recognized as cornfields, farmers, and nothing to do. It now hosts large national events and offers hundreds of great eateries, breweries, coffeehouses, and more. Des Moines is a hub for adventure and experiences. No matter who you are or what experience you are trying to achieve, you will be able to plan a Des Moines itinerary that will make you want to come back for more.

I have so much joy when I open my inbox and find messages from followers looking for something to do, and I typically can gather more than a few days' worth of ideas to keep them busy. Let this book be a stepping stone to your adventures in Des Moines, Iowa.

Adventureland Amusement Park

ACKNOWLEDGMENTS

Thank you to my family and friends who stick by me every day when I get crazy ideas including quitting my full-time job to jump all in as a blogger. Des Moines Parent has brought so many amazing opportunities I never would have imagined. I am grateful to all my followers and cheerleaders who show up daily to the website and on social media to learn about all the fun happening in Des Moines and through the Midwest. Thank you to everyone who has mentioned my name in a room and/ or connected me with someone who has opened another door of possibilities. Finally, thank you to my husband, Travis, and my two children, Monte and Amelia. I am grateful to have them by my side on this wonderful journey traveling, exploring, and experiencing unique opportunities.

The Slow Down Coffee Co.

FOOD
AND DRINK

CATCH A WAVE FOR BREAKFAST
AT WAVELAND CAFE

There is no better way to start a day of exploration than stuffing your stomach with a fulfilling breakfast. Des Moines offers several great breakfast spots, but nothing beats the best hash browns in the galaxy. Waveland Cafe has famously claimed that title, and this hole-in-the-wall breakfast spot is a must-visit. This Des Moines tradition has been around since 1992, and most weekends you will more than likely have to wait, but it will be worth it. When you walk in you're welcomed by the staff and immediately feel like family in this mom-and-pop café. All items are fresh to order from sauces to soups. They offer all the classics (and large portions) such as an omelet, biscuits and gravy (with huge chunks of sausage), or cinnamon French toast.

4708 University Ave., 515-279-4341
desmoines.wavelandcafe.com

TIP
Keep your eyes out for Aquaman, a.k.a. Jason Momoa, who visits the café regularly when traveling home to the Des Moines area.

STEP BACK IN TIME
AT LIVING HISTORY FARMS

Go back a century in time for a 1900 farmhouse dinner at Living History Farms. When you arrive at the farms, a horse-drawn wagon will carry you to the farmhouse for a delicious, authentic meal with items like roasted chicken, sage stuffing, and corn and tomato casserole. You'll be seated around a cozy, intimate table with 10 close friends and you will dine family style. Not only will you indulge in a meal cooked on a wood-burning stove, but you'll enjoy a dinner show as well. All meals are cooked and served by historic interpreters who will share stories and details of how others would have dined in that time period. Finish the evening with chocolate cake and fruit pie during a lantern-lit trip outside to the historic barn to visit horses and other farm animals. This is definitely an experience you will remember for a lifetime. Take note: reservations are required.

11121 Hickman Rd., Urbandale, 515-278-5286
lhf.org

TIP

Visit Living History Farms on Saturdays or Sundays during the holiday season to participate in a Victorian tea, served by staff dressed in attire from the 1870s.

ENJOY
A GOREMET BURGER
AT ZOMBIE BURGER

Who knew it would be so much fun to eat burgers and drink shakes with zombies? Zombie Burger and Drink Lab is located in downtown Des Moines and is a fun spot for lunch or dinner for all ages. Their burgers and shakes are considered fast food with options to sit down and eat or grab a meal to go from their quick-service counter. Zombie Burger is known for using only the best and freshest ingredients and was voted the Best Burger in Iowa by the Daily Meal. Their burgers have unique names such as Juan of the Dead, 28 Days Later, or (my favorite) Undead Elvis. Do not forget to order an over-the-top specialty shake with your meal, and if you are dining in, make it boozy. One of our favorite shakes is the Zombie Unicorn, which includes marshmallow cream and Fruity Pebbles to bring out the child in everyone. Enjoy the fun decor, and make sure you take at least one picture with a zombie.

300 E Grand Ave., 515-244-9292
zombieburgerdm.com

SIP ON AN IOWA BEER
AT THE IOWA TAPROOM

Beer lovers unite at the Iowa Taproom! Take a seat at the 1880s bar-top salvaged from a bar in Jewell and choose from hundreds of Iowa beers from the large, metal Sukup silo that is the main focus of the taproom. This bar and restaurant not only serve up local brews and amazing food but also a building and decor rich in history. The 1882 East Village building was used originally to make commercial door fixtures. From 1916 to 1930, the building held Hawkeye Cord Tire Company, the very first company in Iowa to produce automotive tires! As you sip on your beer, take a look around the building. You may see reclaimed wood that makes up the chunky tables or a switchboard from the Randolph Hotel, which serves at the hostess stand.

215 E 3rd St., Ste. 100, 515-243-0827
iowataproom.com

TIP

Not interested in beer? Head to the lower level to Ken's, a not-so-secret speakeasy where the room is full of Templeton Rye and Cedar Ridge Whiskey barrels; they serve up tasty cocktails including a killer old-fashioned. While sipping on your drink, you can enjoy swing, jazz, vintage covers, and more.

TRY
A MIDWEST STEAK DISH SPECIALTY

Steaks can be cooked in all different ways, but if you are in Des Moines, you will want to try the Steak de Burgo. The Steak de Burgo was originally created in Des Moines and consists of a beef tenderloin topped with butter, garlic, and Italian herbs. It melts in your mouth, and once you have indulged in one, you won't go back. A lot of restaurants in the Des Moines area claim to have the best Steak de Burgo, but our personal favorite can be found at Simon's. Simon's is a small Italian restaurant that is open just in the evenings and typically has a wait out the door. You'll love the intimate setting and, of course, all the delicious food—including the Steak de Burgo.

If you don't make it to Simon's to try the Midwest specialty, check out one of these other great restaurants that offer the classic.

Simon's
5800 Franklin Ave., 515-255-3725
simonsdsm.com

Baratta's Restaurant
2320 S Union St., 515-243-4516
barattas.com

Chicago Speakeasy
1520 Euclid Ave., 515-243-3141
chicagospeakeasyrestaurant.com

Johnny's Italian Steakhouse
6800 Fleur Dr., 515-287-0847
johnnysitaliansteakhouse.com/des-moines

ENJOY HIP-HOP FLAVOR
AT EGGS & JAM

Jump back in time with the Funky Bunch, Snoop Dogg, and Lisa "Left Eye" Lopes, and enjoy breakfast or lunch at Des Moines's only hip-hop-themed restaurant. The vibe and decor are as much of a reason to visit as the hip-hop flavor they serve up. When you walk in, you'll be welcomed with floor-to-ceiling murals of hip-hop artists from the '90s in bright colors. As you look over your food and drink menu, you can head-bob to DMX, Tupac, and more. The food and drinks are cherries on top. Sip on a Still Not a Playa (champagne and your choice of juice) or order the Yo Homes to Bel Air omelet or egg rolls named You Can Touch This. As you can tell, the menu is filled with tributes to legends from the hip-hop era.

1907 EP True Pkwy., Ste. 102, West Des Moines, 515-528-2248
eggsandjamwdm.com

GET REAL CHEESY
AT THE CHEESE BAR

Des Moines may not be the cheese state, but you can find some of the best cheeses from around the world at the Cheese Bar and the Cheese Shop. Owners C. J. and Kari Bienert offer more than 100 artisan and farmhouse cheeses and are extremely knowledgeable in their history and production. While cheese is their forte, they also have a passion to bring the community together. Enjoy a more intimate setting with wine and other cheese accompaniments, or purchase everything you need to create your own charcuterie board at the Cheese Shop. Take a seat at the Cheese Bar and enjoy an over-the-top grilled cheese or cast-iron mac and cheese. They also serve cocktails and local brews. Definitely a spot for some comfort food!

The Cheese Bar
2925 Ingersoll Ave., 515-277-7828
cheesebardsm.com

The Cheese Shop
833 42nd St., 515-528-8181
thecheeseshopdsm.com

PUT A PEP IN YOUR STEP
WITH COFFEE

Before you head into Des Moines to shop or explore the parks, you'll need some fuel to kick-start your day. The Des Moines area is blessed with local coffee shops that serve up delicious lattes and breakfast treats, and many even roast their own beans. One local coffee shop, Smokey Row Coffee Co., has become so popular they now offer several locations across the Des Moines metro. They serve coffee, breakfast, lunch, and ice cream options. Blue Bean Coffee offers flights where you can sample different lattes in one sitting. Head to the historic Highland Park Neighborhood to slow down with friends at the Slow Down Coffee Co., where you'll find local artists' works on the walls, regular community events, and tasty treats from local bakers. If you enjoy four-legged, furry friends while you drink your cup of joe, Coffee Cats allows you to sip your drink and play with cats from the local animal shelter.

Smokey Row Coffee Co.
1910 Cottage Grove Ave., 515-244-2611
smokeyrow.com

Horizon Line Coffee
1417 Walnut St., Ste. B, 515-244-0059
horizonlinecoffee.com

The Slow Down Coffee Co.
3613 6th Ave., 515-630-7000
theslowdowndsm.com

Blue Bean
110 N Ankeny Blvd., Ste. 200, Ankeny, 515-207-9998
bluebean.studio/coffee

The Coffeesmith
770 SE Alice's Rd., Waukee, 515-447-5137
yourcoffeesmith.com

Coffee Cats
312 5th St., West Des Moines, 515-897-5410
coffeecatscafe.com

Northern Vessel
1201 Keosauqua Way, 515-612-8283
nv.coffee

Porch Light Coffeehouse
417 SW 3rd St., Ankeny, 515-499-9999
porchlightcoffeehouse.com

Scenic Route Bakery
350 E Locust St., Ste. 104, 515-288-0004
scenicroutebakerydsm.com

ENJOY
A SPECIALTY COCKTAIL
AT A COCKTAIL BAR

If you are looking for a fun vibe and creative cocktails, Des Moines has several cocktail bars. Hello, Marjorie serves up fun house cocktails including the Weekend Layover and Praline on a Dream. Grab a social-media-worthy picture in front of their infamous *The Prettiest Girls in the World Live in Des Moines* neon sign. Then head to the back of Hello, Marjorie and enjoy an experiment-focused cocktail parlor that requires reservations. During the holiday season, the bar is festively decorated and visitors can enjoy the Naughty List of holiday-themed cocktails. Reservations sell out quickly! For your next round, head to the Bellhop, where it's always tropical in Des Moines. Enjoy tiki-inspired drinks such as the Funky Flamingo or Narcoma Paloma. If you have a big group, you can indulge in one of their shared tiki bowls.

Hello, Marjorie
717 Locust St., 515-369-2296
hellomarjorie.com

Good News, Darling
717 Locust St., 515-369-2296
exploretock.com/good-news-darling

Secret Admirer
110 SW 5th St.
secretadmirerdsm.com

The New Northwestern Cocktail & Wine Bar
321 E Walnut St., 515-410-1423
thenewnorthwestern.com

Bellhop
440 E Grand Ave.
bellhoptikidsm.com

The Bartender's Handshake
3615 Ingersoll Ave., 515-630-3008
thebartendershandshake.com

EXPERIENCE AN AGRIHOOD
AT MIDDLEBROOK FARM

Middlebrook Farm, located just south of Des Moines, is Iowa's first "agrihood." Instead of building large cities on farmland, agrihood preserves the land around it for farming and gardening. Middlebrook brings neighborhoods together and supports the community with healthy food and family. You don't need to live within Middlebrook to experience this small community. It offers a farm with a farm stand available for self-service Monday through Saturday. Make a trip on a Friday evening in the summer to experience Fridays at the Farm, which include live music, beautiful landscapes, and many vendors. You can also shop the Middlebrook Mercantile or play at Middlebrook Park, which is farm themed.

Cumming Ave./Hwy. G14, Cumming, 515-309-0705
middlebrookfarm.com

ENJOY A SWEET TREAT
AT SNOOKIES MALT SHOP

When the temperatures begin warming up in Des Moines, natives begin counting down the days for this classic ice cream shop located in the Beaverdale neighborhood to open its doors and windows for the season. Since 1986, Snookies Malt Shop has been serving some of the best soft-serve ice cream. On most summer nights, the entire property is filled with families in line to snag their favorite ice cream treat. There are benches and seating all around the shop, including swinging wooden benches that families love to sit on while enjoying their treats. Some known favorites include peanut parfaits, chocolate malts, crunch cones, an arctic blast, or even a pup cone for your furry friend.

1810 Beaver Ave., 515-255-0638

GRAB A SWEET GIFT
AT CHOCOLATE STORYBOOK

Chocolate lovers, rejoice! There is nothing better than a local, handmade confection, and since 1986, Chocolate Storybook has been making handmade chocolates. Each is carefully crafted with love and care. They take pride in using only the best ingredients including fresh country cream, real chocolate, real butter, fruits, nuts, and more. Unlike many candies in the industry that include additives, you won't find any extras in their chocolates. Grab some sweets for yourself or an entire gift basket for a loved one. This local chocolate shop is also known for creating logo chocolates, which are a great gift idea for businesses. Not a chocolate fan? They also make caramels from scratch by slow cooking in an open copper kettle. Check out the newer Fairy Tale Cotton Candy with fun flavors such as root beer float, maple bacon, spicy pickle, and more.

1000 Grand Ave., West Des Moines, 515-226-9893
chocolatestory.com

ENJOY PARADISE IN THE MIDDLE OF DES MOINES
AT CAPTAIN ROY'S

The Des Moines River runs through the heart of Des Moines, so why not enjoy a little oasis of food, drink, and fun right along the water? Captain Roy's is just that. When you sit outside along the water and take in the scenery, you quickly forget you are even in the middle of a big town. The restaurant offers a giant outdoor patio, an indoor option where you can grab drinks from the bar, and a bus where all the food is cooked. They serve typical bar food such as the Bus Burger, cheese curds, patty melts, and more. You can easily access this gem by bike because it is right off the bike trail or by boat because they offer docks. Interested in getting on the water? They also offer kayaking options.

1900 Saylor Rd., 515-631-2223
captainroys.com

TIP
Head here for lunch or dinner after a ride on the Heritage Carousel located right up the hill from Captain Roy's.

RELAX WITH A COLD ONE
AT A DES MOINES BREWERY

Des Moines has no shortage of local breweries. Each one offers a little something different that keeps you coming back for more. Court Avenue Restaurant & Brewing Company (also referred to as CABCo) is located in the Saddlery Building in downtown Des Moines. In 1996 it was the very first brewery in Des Moines since Prohibition. Today they serve great food and beer. Kinship is mostly known for their dog park and large patio, and Confluence (located just south of Gray's Lake off the bike path) welcomes bikers. If you are a fan of sour beer and love to try some unconventional types of brews, head to Barn Town Brewing and try a Pickle Tickle. During the colder months, they also offer igloos for a fun experience outdoors. No matter your beer preference, you are sure to find something you will like and a fun experience at one of the many breweries in the area.

Court Avenue Restaurant & Brewing Company
309 Court Ave., 515-282-2739
courtavebrew.com

Kinship Brewing Company
255 NW Sunrise Dr., Waukee
kinshipbeer.com

Confluence Brewing Company
1235 Thomas Beck Rd., 515-285-9005
confluencebrewing.com

Barn Town Brewing
9500 SE University Ave., West Des Moines, 515-978-6767
barntownbrewing.com

Firetrucker Brewery
716 SW 3rd St., Ankeny, 515-964-1284
firetrucker.com

Exile Brewing Company
1514 Walnut St., 515-883-2337
exilebrewing.com

CHALLENGE YOURSELF
AT JETHRO'S BBQ

Are you ready for a challenge? Take the Adam Emmenecker Challenge at Jethro's BBQ; this mammoth sandwich was featured on *Man v. Food* with Adam Richman, who failed the challenge. This four-pound sandwich consists of a cheddar cheeseburger, bacon, brisket, fried cheese, buffalo chicken tenders, cheese sauce, one pound of waffle fries, and a spicy pickle to top it off. Named after Drake University basketball player Adam Emmenecker, this giant meal consists of all of Emmenecker's favorite foods. Emmenecker was a regular at the original Jethro's BBQ that was located in the Drake neighborhood. If you want to take part in the challenge, you have to eat the entire sandwich and fries within 15 minutes. Not interested in the challenge? Try the sandwich without a time limit. I recommend splitting it with friends! You can order it on its own at any of the seven Jethro's locations in Des Moines. Each location offers a different theme including seafood, jambalaya, steaks, or breakfast.

Jethro's BBQ Lakehouse
1425 SW Vintage Pkwy., Ankeny, 515-289-4444
ankeny.jethrosdesmoines.com

Jethro's BBQ Jambalaya
9350 University Ave., West Des Moines, 515-987-8686
waukee.jethrosdesmoines.com

Jethro's BBQ Pork Chop Grill
5950 NW 86th St., Johnston, 515-421-4848
porkchopgrill.jethrosdesmoines.com

Jethro's BBQ Bacon Bacon
1480 22nd St., West Des Moines, 515-868-0888
westdesmoines.jethrosdesmoines.com

Jethro's BBQ Southside
4337 Park Ave., 515-630-6374
southside.jethrosdesmoines.com

Jethro's N Jake's Smokehouse Steaks
2601 Adventureland Dr., Altoona, 515-957-9727
altoona.jethrosdesmoines.com

Jethro's BBQ Ames
1301 Buckeye Ave., Ames, 515-598-1200
ames.jethrosdesmoines.com

INDULGE IN SOME ICE CREAM NUGGETS
AT BLACK CAT ICE CREAM

Black Cat Ice Cream is not your typical ice cream shop. They are known for thinking outside of the box with their flavors, including the Killer Bee. This unique treat is made up of honey and habanero ice cream with burnt sugar and was named best ice cream flavor in the Midwest by the North American Ice Cream Association. Owner Alex Carter is a pastry chef and has been featured on Food Network's *Chopped Sweets*, which has led him to get really creative. To take it up a notch, Black Cat offers ice cream nuggets. Think chicken nuggets, but with ice cream! They regularly create new concoctions such as peanut butter chocolate chip ice cream, dipped in peanut butter and breaded in Cocoa Puffs, served with a tasty sauce on the side. Just as the name describes, you will enjoy their wall dedicated to customers' black cats and a fun patio with a large mural where you can enjoy your treat.

2511 Cottage Grove Ave., 515-689-7466
blackcaticecream.com

TAKE A SIP
OF FRESH, CRISP APPLES
AT WINTERSET CIDERY

Just west of Des Moines is a little piece of heaven. The Winterset Cidery sits on the rolling hills of the Midwest. Come for the cider or for the views; you will not want to leave. The building is located right next to the apple orchard that grows several types of apples, and visitors are encouraged to walk through the orchard, relax, and take in the scenery. All ciders are made fresh from their apples or sourced from other apples in the Midwest. No sugar, water, or artificial flavors or ingredients are ever added. They offer fun and unique hard cider flavors including apple pie, lime habanero, guava, and more. Each year there are different flavors depending on the apples. Plan your visit when they have live music and other fun events during their seasonal opening, which is early May through fall.

1638 Hwy. 169, Winterset, 515-493-9756
wintersetcidery.com

TIP
Bring your folding chairs, blankets, a ball, and a picnic lunch. You can enjoy your cider while sitting out on the grounds or playing a game.

ENJOY
A FRESH IOWA DINNER
AT THE WALLACE HOUSE

The Wallaces are considered the first family of agriculture and planted roots in Iowa just outside of Des Moines. Today, the Wallace Centers of Iowa consist of the Wallace House in Des Moines and Wallace Farm just outside of Des Moines in Orient. The organization continues the work of the Wallace family by connecting people to food and the land. There are many ways they do this work, including cooking classes, growing produce for food-insecure Iowans, offering historic teas, and more. One popular event is the seasonal Farm to Table Thursdays. These dinners are hosted at the Wallace House in Sherman Hill and feature fresh ingredients grown out on the farm and served by a local chef. Guests will enjoy an entire three-course meal inspired by what is available on the farm with a description of each dish by the chef. A wonderful way to enjoy some Iowa history, delicious food, and fun atmosphere!

756 16th St., 515-243-7063
wallace.org

TIP

The Wallace Farm is open to the public year-round and open daily for visitors to tour the grounds any time of the day or evening. Plan a visit on a Friday during the summer and enjoy Pizza on the Prairie, where they use local produce to create delicious handmade brick-oven pizzas and have live music.

GRAB A SLICE OF PIE
IN DES MOINES

Whether you like deep dish, wood grilled, fancy ingredients, or just cheese, Des Moines has you covered when it comes to pizza. Since 1975, Felix & Oscar's has been serving their famous deep-dish pizza and is a great place for families to dine in and enjoy a Sunday family dinner. Big Tomato Pizza Co. has been voted best pizza 10 years in a row and serves pizzas with any ingredient imaginable, including hot dogs, Cajun shrimp, and more. If it's a late night, they are the place to call! They deliver to almost anywhere in Des Moines until 3 a.m. Chuck's Restaurant has been known since 1956 for their pizza made and baked in their storefront window and their Italian American entrées. It is one of the oldest restaurants in the city of Des Moines. Fong's Pizza adds an Asian, Italian, and Polynesian twist on pizza and includes specialty pies such as the Crab Rangoon, Ramen Pizza, or Fongolian Beef.

Felix & Oscar's
4050 Merle Hay Rd., 515-278-8887
felixandoscars.com

Big Tomato Pizza Co.
2613 Ingersoll Ave., 515-288-7227
bigtomatopizza.com

Chuck's Restaurant
3610 6th Ave., 515-381-3118
chucksdsm.com

Fong's Pizza
223 4th St., 515-323-3333
fongspizza.com

Gusto Pizza Bar
2301 Ingersoll Ave., 515-244-8786
gustopizzaco.com

EXPERIENCE UPSCALE DINING
AT 801 CHOPHOUSE

There's a reason 801 Chophouse claims to be the "best fine dining in downtown Des Moines." That's in part because the restaurant, located in the heart of downtown, only serves prime USDA steaks paired with innovative side dishes and an array of wines from around the world. All this and more—including beautiful views, tasty appetizers like "down home" sautéed jumbo shrimp, and yummy pastry desserts—culminates in an upscale, fine-dining experience. Be sure to book a reservation, though, because it's no secret how great this place is. And if you're looking to host a party, 801 Chophouse offers four private dining rooms that can fit up to 48 people comfortably. Oh, and even though you may have visited another 801 Chophouse location in the past (they have a few around the Midwest), we're pretty biased and think Des Moines has the best.

801 Grand Ave., Ste. 200, 515-288-6000
801chophouse.com/des-moines

GRAB A MIDDAY PICK-ME-UP TREAT
AT LA MIE BAKERY

La Mie Bakery dubs itself as Des Moines's favorite neighborhood bakery. That's because their food and drinks are good . . . really good. For a pick-me-up, you can choose from their cold-brew coffee or a matcha green tea latte or even one of their decadent iced chocolate chai lattes. You can also gear up for a big day with their veggie scrambles or an avocado croissant. Then there are La Mie's salads that are a great go-to lunch option, or even try one of their artisan pizzas, which include options like buffalo chicken or meat supreme. Folks working downtown can enjoy the convenience of La Mie Elevate, located in the skywalk. Their main location is located a short distance away at 841 42nd Street. Get ready for a great day with La Mie!

841 42nd St., 515-255-1625
lamiebakery.com

HAVE A QUICK LUNCH
AT ONE OF DES MOINES'S MANY FOOD TRUCKS

Food trucks have become a big deal just about everywhere, and that's no different for Des Moines. In fact, in the summer, the Des Moines Partnership celebrates these mobile eateries with its Out to Lunch Series—a free event open to the public, designed to create a unique and fun opportunity for downtown Des Moines employees, residents, and visitors to socialize with others while enjoying local food trucks and live music. Out to Lunch is held every Wednesday from 11 a.m. to 1:30 p.m. throughout the summer at various locations around Des Moines. With so many amazing options, it's hard to narrow down the best of the best food trucks in the area, but here are a few standout ones: Top Bun, Flame New American Cuisine, the Big Red Food Truck, Roadside Tacos, Wingz on Wheelz, the Outside Scoop, and so many more.

dsmpartnership.com/downtowndsmusa/experiencing-downtown/
festivals-and-markets/out-to-lunch

START YOUR DAY WITH SOME FUN
AT THE BREAKFAST CLUB

The Breakfast Club launched its first Des Moines location in the East Village a few years ago. It grew in popularity so quickly that an additional metro location opened in West Glen a couple years later. Now, there are plans for even more locations to open around the metro. It's obvious what a great brunch option the Breakfast Club is. From s'more donut holes to breakfast corn dogs to stuffed French toast, we're only getting started. There's also creatively named main dishes like Never Benny Better (the Breakfast Club's take on eggs Benedict) and Lox of Love (which features a piece of rye bread loaded with smoked salmon, cream cheese, and more). They've also got a selection of burgers and sandwiches for our breakfast-adverse friends. Of course, top everything off with one of the Breakfast Club's famous cocktails, like their bloody Mary or an espresso martini. Expect to have nothing but a good time here on your next brunch outing.

The Breakfast Club East Village
212 E 3rd St., 515-280-5251

The Breakfast Club West Glen
5525 Mills Civic Pkwy., #100, West Des Moines, 515-224-7030

thebreakfastclubusa.com

Monsterama

MUSIC
AND ENTERTAINMENT

ENJOY THE OUTDOORS
AT JASPER WINERY

Add live outdoor music by local artists to bountiful local wine and you have a perfect summer evening in Des Moines. Every Thursday evening beginning in mid-May through mid-August, Jasper Winery hosts a summer concert series. Jasper is a local winery set up in the heart of Des Moines, but you quickly forget you are in town when you enter their beautiful vineyard. The concert series is a free event for the community where anyone and everyone (age 21 and older, of course) is invited to sip on wines, play yard games, listen to live music from local artists, dance, and more. Grab your favorite food on your way, bring a lawn chair or a blanket, and spend the evening outdoors with friends. If you forget to grab food, don't worry: they offer grilled brats, burgers, and other food truck options depending on the week.

2400 George Flagg Pkwy., 515-282-9463
jasperwinery.com

TIP
If you don't make it to the summer concert series, you can drop into the winery during their business hours and sample wines any time of the year.

SUPPORT THE DES MOINES FILM COMMUNITY
AT THE VARSITY CINEMA

The building where today's Varsity Cinema sits was first built in 1917. It holds a ton of rich history; even before it was a theater, it housed the Coca-Cola bottling plant. The Varsity Cinema opened on Christmas Day in 1938. In 2020, the building was named a Landmark Building by the City of Des Moines Landmark Board and recently underwent a massive renovation. Today, the nonprofit Des Moines Film runs this community art house cinema in the Drake neighborhood and supports both film lovers and aspiring filmmakers. The theater offers one main theater, concessions, and a smaller loft theater. Moviegoers can see international movies, kids and family series, old classics such as *Singin' in the Rain*, and more.

1207 25th St., 515-259-0167
varsitydesmoines.com

EAT, PLAY, AND DRINK
AT SMASH PARK

Smash Park is a whole new level of entertainment with a focus on pickleball. Whether you're a pro or a novice, this large entertainment facility will meet you where you are in this trendy sport. If you're planning a family game night, a friends' night out, or a date night, Smash Park has everything you need. They are known for their indoor and outdoor pickleball courts, but they also offer large yard games, board games, arcade games, great food, and fun drinks for all. Looking to catch the big game? Smash Park offers live watch parties on their 30-foot TV wall and more than 80 TVs. Before heading to this entertainment venue, take a look at their event schedule: they regularly offer community events such as trivia night or bingo.

6625 Coachlight Dr., West Des Moines, 515-313-0700
smashpark.com/west-des-moines

ENJOY WORLD-CLASS ENTERTAINMENT AND CULTURE
WITH DES MOINES PERFORMING ARTS

You don't need to travel to the Big Apple to enjoy a Broadway show and other fine arts. Des Moines Performing Arts offers four venues in downtown Des Moines to experience live shows and music, including the Temple Theater, Des Moines Civic Center, Stoner Stage, and Cowles Commons. The Temple Theater is located on the second floor of the Temple for Performing Arts. The setting is more intimate, allowing the audience to feel more a part of the show. The Des Moines Civic Center welcomes all shows for audiences from families to adults, including Broadway hits such as *The Lion King*, *Wicked*, *Cats*, *Rent*, and more. Cowles Commons is an outdoor venue that is home to the familiar *Crusoe Umbrella* by artist Claes Oldenburg. This area hosts outdoor events and is a fun place for families to splash and play in the Lauridsen Fountain during the summer months.

221 Walnut St., 515-246-2300
desmoinesperformingarts.org

SUPPORT
THE COMMUNITY'S
RISING STARS
AT THE DES MOINES PLAYHOUSE

Cheer on rising stars in the theater at the Des Moines Playhouse. Originally named the Little Theater, the Des Moines Playhouse has been around for more than 100 years of uninterrupted entertainment and is one of the largest community theaters in the United States. Today the Playhouse occupies the old Roosevelt Theatre in Des Moines and puts on numerous live productions per year, showcasing casts from the Des Moines community. The Playhouse contains two theaters including Kate Goldman's Children's Theatre, which produces four shows each year specifically geared toward families. Past productions include *Harriet the Spy*, *Charlotte's Web*, and other children's favorites. The John Viars Theatre produces a variety of shows including Broadway hits such as *Guys and Dolls*, *Little Shop of Horrors*, and many other favorites.

831 42nd St., 515-277-6261
dmplayhouse.com

CATCH THE BIGGEST NAMES ON THE BIGGEST STAGE
AT IOWA EVENTS CENTER

Catch a hockey game, see a big act, or discover larger-than-life dinosaurs at the Iowa Events Center in downtown Des Moines. The Iowa Events Center is a three-venue, multipurpose complex made up of Wells Fargo Arena, Hy-Vee Hall, and Community Choice Credit Convention Center. Wells Fargo Arena is home to the Iowa Wolves basketball team and the Iowa Wild hockey team. The arena has also welcomed many big names such as Faith Hill, Tim McGraw, the Eagles, and more. In 2016, the Iowa Events Center welcomed the third round of the NCAA men's basketball tournament, putting Des Moines on the map for sports fans. In addition, the two convention centers host large family events such as Jurassic Quest, home and garden shows, Festival of Trees and Lights, and large luncheons annually.

730 3rd St., 515-564-8000
iowaeventscenter.com

JAM OUT
AT WOOLY'S

Catch a diverse act in an intimate venue at Wooly's. Since 2012, Wooly's has welcomed genre-diverse musical acts and fans to the East Village. Past bands to visit have included Ice Nine Kills, Andrew McMahon, Ben Rector, Jade Bird, Grouplove, and the Struts. The venue is not overly large and only holds 683 people, which makes it the perfect place to learn about new bands and catch a front-row seat. The venue makes for an intimate experience with the artists. Get to know local bands and jam out to cover bands. Wooly's has a full lineup with shows nearly every night of the week, so there are countless opportunities to catch your favorite band . . . or perhaps even something new. Catch dinner in the East Village beforehand and make a whole night of it.

504 E Locust St., 515-244-0550
firstfleetconcerts.com/first-fleet-venues/woolys

LISTEN TO
A LIVE JAZZ SHOW
AT NOCE

Did you know Des Moines gets some amazing jazz performers to come to town? Noce, Des Moines's premier home for jazz, chic events, and classic cocktails, is largely to blame. The all-ages jazz and cabaret club opened on Walnut Street in late 2015. It's owned by arts supporter Maria Reveiz along with vocalist/producer Max Wellman. Noce offers live entertainment Thursday through Saturday evenings, sometimes with another night sprinkled in. There are also performances by the Des Moines Big Band during their Wednesday night residency. You can rent Noce's private event space called Backstage, too, which is a great option for everything from small get-togethers to large-scale weddings. And fun fact: The venue's house piano, a Boston baby grand crafted by Steinway, has a walnut finish, matching the walnut theme of the venue, which is a nod to the street it's located on.

1326 Walnut St., 515-244-5399
nocedsm.com

FOLLOW THE TWINKLY LIGHTS FOR A GOOD CAUSE
AT JOLLY HOLIDAY LIGHTS

Every holiday season Make-A-Wish® Iowa puts on Jolly Holiday Lights, its largest fundraiser, which raises money to grant wishes to children who have been affected by a critical illness. On average, this event grants approximately 80 wishes per year. What used to be a drive-through light show is now moving to a new format after 27 years. Attendees are able to enjoy the lights, music, the Wish Shop, and special events that all continue to raise money for Make-A-Wish®. You can find this new experience at Outlets of Des Moines in a more immersive experience that kicks off with a tree lighting with Santa and a Wish child in mid-November. Some events include breakfast with Santa, sip & shop, and more.

3300 Adventureland Dr.
jollyholidaylights.org

GO CAMPING
AT HINTERLAND MUSIC FESTIVAL

A huge music festival . . . in the middle of a field . . . in Iowa? Yep, that's right. The Hinterland Music Festival is a multiday celebration that features artists ranging from the famed to the up and coming. Located outside the tiny town of St. Charles, which is just south of Des Moines, Hinterland attracts visitors from far and wide. Some folks choose to camp at the festival's campground while others come and go for the day. The good news is that the festival is also kid-friendly. There's even a special Hinterkids tent that runs activities throughout the festival, like arts and crafts and face painting. The festival happens in early August with tickets going on sale earlier in the year, so keep an eye out for each year's incredible (trust us!) lineup.

3357 St. Charles Rd., St. Charles
hinterlandiowa.com

ROCK OUT TO DIVERSE MUSIC
AT 80/35 MUSIC FESTIVAL

Another summer music festival famous to Des Moines is 80/35. The multiday festival gets its name from the two major interstates that intersect in Des Moines. The main stage features national touring bands, while several smaller stages highlight regional and local acts. In the past, notable acts have included Liz Phair, Phoebe Bridgers, Nas, Wilco, and Ziggy Marley. 80-35 started in 2008, and it's estimated that the festival brings an attendance of more than 30,000 people each year. It's also nearly 100 percent volunteer run and organized by the Greater Des Moines Music Coalition, which is committed to building a stronger and more diverse live music economy in Des Moines. 80-35 is held in Western Gateway Park, so visitors who stop by the festival can also enjoy all that downtown has to offer.

1205 Locust St.
80-35.com

CELEBRATE THE FOURTH OF JULY
AT YANKEE DOODLE POPS

Every Fourth of July, the Des Moines Symphony welcomes more than 100,000 Iowans to celebrate the nation's birthday at the family-friendly, patriotic concert Yankee Doodle Pops. This is the largest single-day concert event in Iowa; it includes many vendors and one of the biggest fireworks displays over the downtown Des Moines skyline. Iowans gather snacks, lawn chairs, and blankets and head to the steps of the Iowa Capitol to listen and celebrate the nation's birthday. The concert kicks off with the winner of the Des Moines Symphony's "Oh Say, Can You Sing?" competition, who sings "The Star-Spangled Banner." You do not need to physically attend to hear the music and see the fireworks. In partnership with Iowa PBS, Yankee Doodle Pops is also broadcast live across the state.

1007 E Grand Ave.
dmsymphony.org/concerts-events/yankee-doodle-pops

GET YOUR FRIGHT
AT SHERMAN HILL'S
HALLOWEEN ON THE HILL

The oldest neighborhood in Des Moines has a beloved Halloween tradition: Halloween on the Hill. The Sherman Hill neighborhood event was started when a couple of Halloween enthusiasts in the area decorated their homes but also wanted to have a positive impact on those around them. So, they recruited neighbors to join in. Today, the event is a neighborhood-wide celebration of Halloween and community that goes beyond a few hours of trick-or-treating. Front yards are covered in spooky decorations, while traditions like a "Thriller" performance fill the streets and Freddy Krueger roams around. Another tradition is a reading of "The Raven" by Edgar Allan Poe, performed by trained actors on a Victorian porch. The celebrations are free, but attendees are encouraged to bring nonperishable food items or monetary donations for the Des Moines Area Religious Council (DMARC) at one of five locations either before, after, or during the event. When you do, you'll receive a map of the neighborhood's frights and thrills.

16th and 17th Streets and Crocker St. to Woodland Ave.
shermanhilldsm.org

SPEND YOUR DAY
HAVING SOME OLD-SCHOOL ARCADE AND BOWLING FUN

Looking to hit up an arcade or go bowling? The good news is Des Moines has no shortage of options. B&B Theatres, located in Ankeny, is not only a movie theater, but they also offer arcade games and bowling. Your family will have a great time playing air hockey and tons of other arcade fun. Or visit Johnston's new Backpocket Pin & Pixel that offers several retro arcade games, duckpin bowling, and yummy snacks and drinks. There's also the Great Escape, located in Pleasant Hill, which is an entire entertainment complex for all ages. Looking for a fright? Consider the Monsterama Arcade. Here, you'll find vintage '80s and '90s era arcade games, pinball, and classic gaming systems. The popular Smash Park by Jordan Creek Town Center also has tons of board games, pickleball, outdoor yard games, and much more. There's so much fun to be had, so pick a spot and enjoy!

B&B Theatres
1580 SW Market St., Ankeny, 515-423-0979
bbtheatres.com

Backpocket Pin & Pixel
6205 Merle Hay Rd., Johnston, 515-666-1281
backpocketpinandpixel.com

Great Escape
655 NE 56th St., Pleasant Hill, 515-263-1700
bowlero.com/location/great-escape

Monsterama Arcade & Pizzeria
3108 SW 9th St., 515-528-2015
monsteramaarcade.com

Smash Park
6625 Coachlight Dr., West Des Moines, 515-313-0700
smashpark.com/west-des-moines

Climb Iowa

SPORTS
AND RECREATION

PERFORM A TRICK
AT THE LARGEST OPEN SKATE PARK

In May of 2021, Des Moines became home to the largest open skate park in the nation. Lauridsen Skatepark is located in the heart of downtown Des Moines along the Principal Riverwalk next to the Des Moines River. This skate park is 88,000 square feet and offers a promenade, flow bowl, amoeba pool, a well-known skateable art piece entitled WOW, and more. You do not need to be a skateboarder to enjoy this facility. Many bring bikes, roller skates, or rollerblades and take advantage of all the offerings. It is free to skate, but make sure you wear your knee pads, elbow pads, and helmets!

Since Lauridsen Skatepark's opening, the annual Dew Tour competition and festival has been held there, featuring competition from the world's top male and female skateboarders.

901 2nd Ave.
dsmskatepark.com

ENJOY
GORGEOUS IOWA VIEWS
ON THE HIGH TRESTLE TRAIL

Whether you are a devoted bike rider or enjoy more casual bike rides, you do not want to miss the opportunity to ride along the 25-mile-long High Trestle Trail. This path runs across five towns and has many access points, which makes it perfect for any level of rider. This trail was converted from discontinued railroads that ran across the Iowa countryside. After much planning, fundraising, and construction, this is now one of the best spots to take in views of the Des Moines River Valley and even catch a glimpse of a bald eagle flying. The highlight of the trail is the half-mile, 13-story High Trestle Bridge, which lights up at night. If you can only explore a small section of the trail, the bridge is a must-see. If you do not care to bike, skaters and walkers are invited to walk the trail and take in the beautiful scenery.

Trail running from Ankeny to Woodward, 515-288-1846
inhf.org/what-we-do/protection/high-trestle-trail

TIP
For easy access to view the bridge, park at the trailhead located in Madrid just 2.6 miles east of the bridge.

ENJOY
ALL THINGS OUTDOORS
AT JESTER PARK

The Des Moines area offers many wonderful places to take in the outdoors, and one of the most popular destinations is Jester Park. You can easily spend an entire day or weekend taking in all of the activities and attractions this 1,661-acre park has to offer. This large park is located on the west side of Saylorville Lake. You will find a nature center with interactive displays, a golf course, a miniature golf course, an equestrian center, hiking trails, a natural playscape, bison, elk, an outdoor recreation building with boulder climbing and archery, canoeing, snowshoeing, camping, picnic tables, and so much more. No matter the season in Des Moines, Jester Park welcomes you to find something to experience the outdoors.

12130 NW 128th St., Granger, 515-323-5338
polkcountyiowa.gov/conservation/parks-trails/jester-park

TIP

Throughout the year, the park offers many large events and activities including weekly educational events for all ages and levels. Before planning your trip to Jester Park, make sure to take a look at their events calendar.

PUT ME IN, COACH,
AT PRINCIPAL PARK

A bag of peanuts, a cold brew, and Cubbie at Principal Park, formerly known as Sec Taylor Stadium, make for the perfect spring or summer outing in Des Moines. Watch the minor league baseball team the Iowa Cubs play at their home field just outside of downtown Des Moines. You will enjoy the Des Moines skyline, including the Iowa State Capitol and fireworks shows, several nights throughout the season. This triple-A affiliate team of the Chicago Cubs sometimes welcomes Chicago Cubs players such as pitcher Kerry Wood, who made an appearance in 2005, and many Iowa Cubs players end up on the Chicago Cubs roster in the future. Bring the kids! Children will love the large climbing structure and splash pad to play in on a hot summer day.

One Line Dr., 515-243-6111
milb.com/iowa/ballpark

TIP

Each spring, Principal Park opens its doors for an open house. Fans are invited to walk out on the field, tour the stadium, shop for souvenirs, and more before the season starts.

TAKE A THRILL RIDE
AT ADVENTURELAND
AMUSEMENT PARK

Since 1974, Adventureland Amusement Park has been a source of thrills and fun for families. Beginning as just an amusement park, it is now labeled a resort that consists of a hotel, campground, and restaurant. It has become a magnet for tourists all across the Midwest. Families can enjoy thrill rides such as the Monster or Dragon Slayer roller coasters. Those who are not fans of the thrills can enjoy the many family rides offered. After a morning of rides, head over to Adventure Bay to cool off at their water park, which consists of a wave pool, a lazy river, several slides, and more. Throughout the year, Adventureland hosts several special events such as the Scream Park during Halloween season and concerts throughout the summer months.

3200 Adventureland Dr., Altoona, 515-266-2121
adventurelandresort.com

TIP

Get your hand stamped if you decide to leave the park early. You can return the same day! As a great option to save money on food, head outside the park for a picnic or visit one of the neighboring restaurants for lunch.

ENJOY THE OUTDOORS, INDOORS
AT THE GREATER DES MOINES BOTANICAL GARDEN

As you drive through Des Moines, you will notice a large glass dome along the Des Moines River, and if you look more closely you will notice plants, flowers, and other lush greenery under the dome. This is the 12-acre Greater Des Moines Botanical Garden, which was first planted in 1929 and has a rich and long history to where it is today. The Greater Des Moines Botanical Garden is a nonprofit that invites the public to walk through the dome or outdoor gardens to experience all of the plants and flowers. Guests are encouraged to grab lunch at the on-site café, sit and reflect at the Ruan Reflection Garden, or attend one of their special events, such as Dome after Dark or Botanical Blues offered during the winter months.

909 Robert D. Ray Dr., 515-323-6290
dmbotanicalgarden.com

TIP

The Greater Des Moines Botanical Garden offers free admission days throughout the year including Earth Day (everyone is free), Mother's Day (mothers are free), Father's Day (fathers are free), and Veterans Day (veterans are free).

ENJOY
THE BEST DAYS EVER
AT THE IOWA STATE FAIR

The Iowa State Fair first began in 1854 and today is the single largest event in the state of Iowa. If you talk to locals, many plan their vacations and schedules based on the 11-day fair. The Iowa State Fair kicks off with Iowa's largest parade, which begins in downtown Des Moines and ends at the Iowa State Fairgrounds. Each year the Iowa State Fair attracts millions of people from all over to celebrate everything that makes up Iowa, including food, entertainment, agriculture, and more. Families love to visit the Butter Cow, catch a Billy Riley Talent Show, try for a ribbon in hundreds of competitions, ride on carnival rides, or check out the newest Iowa State Fair food concoction. The Iowa State Fair is known for bringing some of the biggest acts to the grandstand, such as Eric Church, Carrie Underwood, Alan Jackson, and many more. Don't leave the fair without a bucket of Barksdale's warm and gooey cookies.

3000 E Grand Ave., 800-545-FAIR
iowastatefair.org

MAKE ZOO FRIENDS
AT THE BLANK PARK ZOO

Since opening in 1966, the Blank Park Zoo has been a destination for families to visit and learn about animals and conservation in Des Moines, and it's the only accredited zoo in the state of Iowa. The zoo sits on 49 acres on the south side of Des Moines—not an overly large zoo, which makes it perfect for families to enjoy and experience everything it has to offer. You will find a little over 100 different animal species including an African lion, sea lions, red pandas, wallabies, and many others. There are plenty of opportunities for visitors to enjoy hands-on experiences such as feeding the giraffes or feeding the several animals located in Kids Kingdom. In addition to interacting with animals, visitors can ride the train or take a ride on the carousel. If you are over 21 years of age, you will not want to miss Zoo Brew, held in June and July each year. It's a fun chance for adults to taste local brews, listen to live music, and visit with the animals.

7401 SW 9th St., 515-285-4722
blankparkzoo.com

LACE UP YOUR SKATES
FOR A TRIP AROUND THE RINK

There are many great places to ice-skate indoors or outdoors in Des Moines, including Brenton Skating Plaza. Lace up your skates and take a trip around the rink while taking in the Des Moines skyline near the Principal Riverwalk. Throughout the winter season, they offer Learn to Skate clinics, opportunities to skate with superheroes and princesses, and more. If you own your own ice skates and want to skate for free, you can skate around a synthetic ice-skating rink at the Johnston Town Center. Not interested in ice-skating outdoors? You can head to the MidAmerican Energy Company RecPlex, a large indoor sports facility located in West Des Moines. They have two indoor ice-skating rinks and offer public skating year-round.

TIP

Valley Ice Plaza is located outside of the Valley Community Center and open to the public for free during the week. They offer free programming, a play place, an open gym, and more for everyone.

Brenton Skating Plaza
520 Robert D. Ray Dr., 515-283-4233
dsm.city/departments/parks_and_recreation-division/places/
brenton_skating_plaza/index.php

Johnston Town Center
6245 Merle Hay Rd., Johnston, 515-727-7768
johnstontowncenter.com/events/synthetic-ice-rink

MidAmerican Energy Co. RecPlex
6500 Grand Ave., West Des Moines, 515-440-4820
therecplex.com/public-skating

Valley Ice Plaza
4444 Fuller Rd., West Des Moines, 515-327-6000
valleycommunity.center

MAKE A BUTTERFLY FRIEND
AT REIMAN GARDENS

Walk through 17 acres of gardens at Iowa State University. Reiman Gardens invites the public to leave technology behind and enjoy the colors, plants, water features, insects, and butterflies in their oasis of 26 distinct gardens. The gardens are open to the public but are also used by Iowa State University students for research and learning. You can simply spend time walking through the gardens, taking in all the beauty, or book a guided tour to learn about the history and horticulture of the gardens. Don't leave the gardens without a stop at the Christina Reiman Butterfly Wing, which is home to approximately 800 live butterflies. If you stop to look around you and hold out your arm, you are more than likely to make a new butterfly friend during your visit.

1407 University Blvd., Ames, 515-294-2710
reimangardens.com

TIP
Visit during the holidays and walk through the Winter Wonderscape light display.

VIEW THE PAINTED SKY
DURING THE NATIONAL
BALLOON CLASSIC

Every August the skies open up and you will see nearly 100 hot-air balloons for the National Balloon Classic. This nine-day event has been held annually for more than 50 years in Indianola at the Memorial Balloon Field. The entire festival is filled with hot-air balloons with bright colors and different shapes. Attendees are encouraged to come each night to watch the balloons launch while listening to live music, watching fireworks, enjoying food and drink, and more. Some popular flights during the festival include the Nite Glow and Dawn Patrol when the balloons take flight at night or early morning hours and glow in the sky. Everyone's favorite is when the balloons fly over the Des Moines skyline one special day during the classic.

15335 Jewell St., Indianola, 515-961-8415
nationalballoonclassic.com

TIP
Bring blankets, lawn chairs, and even a light jacket! It can get chilly as the sun begins to set.

BECOME A FUTURE SCIENTIST
AT THE SCIENCE CENTER OF IOWA

Since 1970, the Science Center of Iowa has been bringing hands-on exhibits, programming, and education to visitors. The science center consists of several permanent exhibits such as Small Discoveries for the littlest future scientists, including a tot town and a bubbles station. The What on Earth? exhibit offers opportunities to come face-to-face with cold-blooded critters native to Des Moines, or a chance to be on live television with a local meteorologist from WHO-HD in their weather studio. Become an architect in the Brick by Brick exhibit where you are challenged to build different structures and can view famous structures built of LEGOs. Do not miss a chance to catch a show on the 50-foot, 360-degree dome planetarium during your visit. The science center regularly welcomes traveling exhibits and offers live programming, kids camps, and more.

401 W Martin Luther King Jr. Pkwy., 515-274-6868
sciowa.org

TIP
Before you go, take a look at their daily schedule to plan your day so you don't miss a fun show.

USE YOUR IMAGINATION AND PLAY
AT THE DES MOINES CHILDREN'S MUSEUM

The Des Moines Children's Museum's focus is on building the foundation of lifelong learning through the power of play. It started with a dream by two local moms a few years ago with a traveling exhibit, which quickly blossomed into a physical location in Des Moines. While the majority who come to play are young children, older children have had just as much fun. The children's museum creates those opportunities for children and their caregivers to play together. The entire museum is a miniature city where kids can deliver mail to mailboxes spread across the museum, climb aboard a fire truck with a pole to slide down, or use their imaginations to build their own structure in the building area. You can become the next doctor by taking care of dolls or going camping with friends. In addition to hands-on exhibits, the museum also offers different programs and events throughout each month.

1551 Valley West Dr., Ste. 108, West Des Moines, 515-218-8344
dsmchildrensmuseum.com

FOOD, DRINK, AND PLAY FOR YOU AND YOUR BEST FRIEND
AT PAWS & PINTS

Your four-legged best friend needs a place to have fun and explore! Paws & Pints is an amusement park for your dog that provides entertainment and fun for canines and humans. This one-of-a-kind establishment offers everything you and your pup may need under one roof, including a restaurant serving delicious food, beer, and cocktails and a coffeehouse with lattes and bagels. Let your furry friend run and play in the off-leash indoor and outdoor dog parks. The indoor park offers large televisions and seating, while the outdoor park offers a walking trail and seating where humans can connect while their dogs play. They regularly plan special events and live music each month. If you are planning a trip, the facility also offers doggy daycare and boarding options.

6218 Willowmere Dr., 515-969-2275
pawsandpintsdsm.com

PICK
THE BIGGEST PUMPKIN
IN THE PATCH

There is no shortage of places to find the perfect big pumpkin. Today, a trip to the pumpkin patch is much more than selecting the biggest or best pumpkin in the patch. Pumpkin patches now provide hours of fun and entertainment during the fall months for visitors. Howell's Pumpkin Patch is well known for their super friendly and cuddly goats. Several times, beginning in spring through the fall, there are opportunities to bottle-feed the goats, do goat yoga, or just play with them. They also offer a bouncing pillow, a corn pit, and more. Center Grove Orchard has a large pumpkin patch, but they are also known for their apple orchards. There is no shortage of apple goodies you can indulge in. You can spend an entire day playing on their jumping pillow, pedaling tractors, going down the large slide, or riding the train.

Howell's Greenhouse and Pumpkin Patch
3145 Howell Ct., Cumming, 515-981-0863
howellsgreenhouseandpumpkinpatch.com

Center Grove Orchard
32835 610th Ave., Cambridge, 515-383-4354
centergroveorchard.com

TAKE IN DES MOINES'S NATURAL BEAUTY
ON A HIKE

Hiking is a great way to take in some of the natural beauty that resides in the heart of Iowa. Des Moines is blessed with many hiking trails, including a variety of difficulties for any experience level. Enjoy the beautiful hickory and oak trees in Iowa's largest urban forest at Brown's Woods or explore Ledges State Park, which offers beautiful views and sandstone ledges and is considered one of Iowa's most unique nature destinations. Plan a visit to Ewing Park during the spring and catch the beautiful lilacs in full bloom as you hike the nature trail. Plan an entire weekend getaway at Jester Park or Ledges State Park, where they offer camping cabins for families to stay and explore the beauty of the park.

Brown's Woods
465 Brown's Woods Dr., West Des Moines
polkcountyiowa.gov/conservation/parks-trails/brown-s-woods

Jester Park
12130 NW 128th St., Granger
polkcountyiowa.gov/conservation/parks-trails/jester-park

Ledges State Park
1515 P Ave., Madrid
iowadnr.gov/places-to-go/state-parks/iowa-state-parks/ledges-state-park

Margo Frankel Woods State Park
6245 NW 2nd St.

Ewing Park
5300 Indianola Ave.
dsm.city/business_detail_T6_R49.php

PLACE A BET
AT PRAIRIE MEADOWS CASINO

You can enjoy live horse racing, slots, and table games at Prairie Meadows Casino. There are plenty of options for entertainment and gambling. Bring your money to win big or visit to watch the horse races on the one-mile racetrack. A popular event for all is the camel, zebra, and ostrich races that happen annually, which is free and geared toward families. Throughout the year they offer many types of events, including sporting, family-friendly, free shows, and more. The Prairie Meadows complex never wants you to have to leave, so they offer an on-site hotel and several restaurants, including the popular AJ's Steakhouse. Many do not know that this Iowa casino runs as a nonprofit, which allows them to give thousands of dollars back to other charitable organizations within the Des Moines community.

One Prairie Meadows Dr., Altoona, 515-967-1000
prairiemeadows.com

WATCH A FUTURE OLYMPIAN COMPETE
AT THE DRAKE RELAYS

Since 1910, Des Moines has hosted the Drake Relays, an outdoor track-and-field event that is considered one of the top in the nation. Every April, thousands of people flock to Drake Stadium to watch the very best athletes compete and maybe even set some world records. Many gold-medal Olympians have competed at the Drake Relays, including Caitlyn Jenner, Carl Lewis, Wilma Rudolph, Karissa Schweizer, Lolo Jones, and many who have continued on to the Olympic Games. Today, the annual event consists of an entire week of activities for the public to participate in, including the Grand Blue Mile, the downtown Des Moines block party, the Beautiful Bulldog Contest, and many more fun activities to celebrate Des Moines and the Drake Relays.

2719 Forest Ave.
godrakebulldogs.com/sports/drake-relays

HOCKEY FAN OR NOT,
CHEER ON THE IOWA WILD

Watch the puck drop at Wells Fargo Arena, home to the Iowa Wild Des Moines hockey team. The Iowa Wild is the affiliate of the NHL's Minnesota Wild and has called Des Moines home since 2013. From October through April, they play several times per month. Go for hockey or go for fun promotions and events. You can attend a game with a postgame concert, see a fireworks show after the game, participate in the Teddy Bear Toss, or bring your lightsaber for Star Wars Night. You do not want to leave a game without giving Crash, their famous mascot, a high five. Whether or not you're a hockey fan, you will be one after you attend an Iowa Wild game.

730 3rd St., 515-564-8700
iowawild.com

FUN FACT
The Iowa Wild has partnered with many Iowa towns to provide free community ice rinks, which make ice-skating accessible all over.

CHALLENGE YOURSELF
AT CLIMB IOWA

There is no need to travel to Colorado to rock climb! Climb Iowa is Iowa's largest indoor climbing and training facility. Since its opening in 2008, they have hosted seven USA Climbing regional championships and have hosted one USA Climbing divisional championship. Who would think that so many Iowans love to climb? More than 200 people of all ages visit to climb every day. Climb Iowa has two different locations in the Des Moines area, together offering 13,000 square feet of climbing and over 200 routes. Everyone is invited and encouraged to climb, from beginners to pros and all abilities. They offer memberships, orientations, kids camps, yoga, and more. Many climb for exercise or for the challenge, but Climb Iowa is all about creating a community.

3605 SE Miehe Dr., Grimes, 515-986-2565
climbiowa.com/grimes

150 E 4th St., 515-244-2565
climbiowa.com/east-village

WALK OR BIKE THE LOOP
AT GRAY'S LAKE PARK

One of the most popular and most talked about parks in the Des Moines area is Gray's Lake Park. Many locals refer to this 166-acre park as simply Gray's Lake, and whatever they call it, they all agree it offers many fun outdoor activities. You will find people biking or walking around the famous Kruidenier Trail, a loop that is just short of two miles around the lake. If you venture onto the trail at night, you will want to make sure to cross over the 1,400-foot-long and 16-foot-wide Kruidenier Trail Bridge that illuminates the dark with multicolored lights. Visitors are encouraged to fish, play on the playground, swim at the beach, or rent a boat. Every summer, Des Moines Parks and Recreation hosts free Yoga in the Park, led by volunteer yoga instructors every Saturday morning right on the lawn at Gray's Lake Park.

2101 Fleur Dr., 515-237-1386
dsm.city/business_detail_T6_R58.php

LEARN MORE ABOUT THE WILD
AT WATER WORKS PARK

Water Works Park is located along the Raccoon River, directly west of Gray's Lake Park, and is one of America's largest urban parks. Not only does this 1,500-acre park offer tons of outdoor recreational activities, but it also serves as a place to educate the public about the quality of water supplies and more. Approximately 1,400 acres of Water Works Park have been designated as "The Wild," which is to be left untouched to allow the ecosystems to provide clean air and water for generations to come. As you walk or bike the trails, you'll notice signs that share more information. In addition, visitors can play on the natural playscape, fish, or enjoy the equestrian trails. For even more fun, many concerts and festivals are held at this park, including at the Lauridsen Amphitheater Killinger Family Stage. During late April through mid-May, the crabapple trees bloom and visitors flock to the Arie den Boer Arboretum, which contains around 300 varieties of crabapple trees.

2201 George Flagg Pkwy., 515-240-7993
dsmwaterworkspark.com

FEEL AT PEACE IN THE IOWA COUNTRY
AT RUSTY STARS ALPACA

Head into Madison County and you will find a small farm where dozens of alpacas live: Rusty Stars Alpaca. This alpaca farm is owned by Aron and Kari Shultz, who have a love for alpacas and educating others about this unique animal. When you arrive, visitors receive a small overview of how to interact with and feed the alpacas. You will enjoy watching how each alpaca has its own personality and how the owners can tell each of them apart by their specific characteristics. Petting their soft wool and watching them along the Iowa countryside makes for a fun yet calming visit. Before giving your kisses goodbye, make a stop at the Alpaca Shop filled with wool hats, socks, and other fun alpaca goodies.

2054 Rustic Ln., Winterset, 515-705-8404
facebook.com/rustystarsalpacas

HOWL
FOR THE IOWA WOLVES

Howling (or cheering) for the Iowa Wolves, formerly known as the Iowa Energy, is fun for all ages! The Iowa Wolves, affiliated with the Minnesota Timberwolves, is the official basketball team of Des Moines and is a part of the G League, the minor league of the NBA. Approximately 50 percent of NBA players get their start within the NBA G League. So when you attend a game at Wells Fargo Arena, you may be watching the next big NBA star playing on the court. On most game nights, there are themes and fun promotions happening, such as Country Night, special concerts, and more. You will also find many players volunteering their time in the community.

730 3rd St., 515-564-8550
iowa.gleague.nba.com

TAKE A STROLL
ALONG THE PRINCIPAL RIVERWALK

In 2013, the 1.2-mile Principal Riverwalk loop trail was completed, connecting the west and east sides of downtown Des Moines. It is a great way to take in the city view and explore multiple attractions downtown. The Des Moines Union Railway Bridge marks the southern point of the loop, and the Iowa Women of Achievement Bridge marks the northern point of the loop. Along the riverwalk, you will find the Brenton Skating Plaza, Simon Estes Amphitheater, Greater Des Moines Botanical Garden, Rotary Riverwalk Park, and more. During the summer you can take the trail to the Downtown Farmers' Market. And keep going to the connected six-mile Des Moines Art Route with 80 works including popular sculptures and murals that make up Des Moines's rich public art.

115 Grand Ave., 515-237-1386
dsm.city/business_detail_T6_R75.php

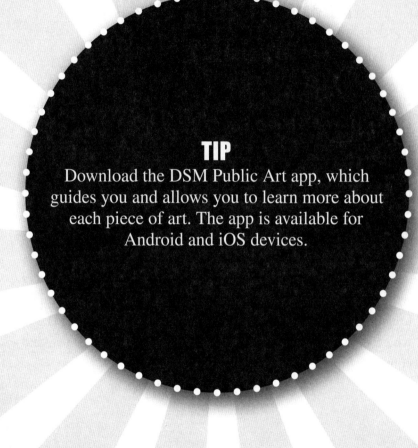

TIP

Download the DSM Public Art app, which guides you and allows you to learn more about each piece of art. The app is available for Android and iOS devices.

PLAY
AT MONTESSORI-INSPIRED JOUJOU DES MOINES

The littlest explorers will enjoy playing and climbing at the Montessori-inspired JouJou Des Moines. This is not your typical indoor play space full of plastic and battery-operated toys. Instead, you will find handmade, wooden toys all encouraging imaginative play. Montessori means a learning approach that focuses on a child's natural interests and abilities, and this is exactly what JouJou supports. The beautiful space is bright, warm, and welcoming with a focus on supporting the local community. In a busy, busy world, this space encourages everyone to slow down and connect. Children and caregivers will enjoy the reading nook where caregivers are encouraged to snuggle up and read. The large gathering table and space is where adults are encouraged to sit down, sip coffee or tea, and connect with others.

906 42nd St., 515-528-2044
joujoudsm.com

GRAB THE BEST VIEW IN THE CITY
AT MACRAE PARK

MacRae Park is a 50-acre city park named after Donald MacRae, the first Iowan killed in World War I, while serving in France. The park was originally called South Park because it is located directly south of downtown Des Moines, and continues to serve that part of town a century later with tons of great outdoor activities for visitors. The most popular attraction is the EMC Overlook, which is 96 feet long, and the tip of the bridge, which hovers 40 feet above the hill! As you look down you can see the river, the Iowa State Capitol, and the Des Moines skyline. Over the years, the park has been through many changes to attract even more visitors, including the addition of a boardwalk over the pond and a custom nature playscape. Some fun things you can enjoy while visiting include the playground, picnic areas, tennis, and fishing.

1021 Davis Ave., 515-237-1386
dsm.city/business_detail_T6_R66.php

ENJOY SOME NOSTALGIA
AT RIVERVIEW PARK

Sometimes referred to as the "island" park, the 44-acre Riverview Park has a rich history dating all the way back to 1889. The park originally was the Des Moines Zoological Gardens, which included an elephant, panthers, monkeys, elk, birds, and more. In 1915, the Riverview Amusement Park opened with admission for five cents and offered several rides, such as the Jack Rabbit Roller Coaster. The attraction stayed open, through several ups and downs, until 1978. Adventureland then purchased Riverview Park with plans to continue operation, but eventually closed it instead. Several rides were moved from Riverview to Adventureland. Today, the park is full of nostalgia with an amusement-themed playground that has a nod to the original, plus a large amphitheater, miles of connected paved trails, and tons of green space. The playground is a Variety Star playground that welcomes all abilities to play.

710 Corning Ave., 515-237-1386
dsm.city/business_detail_T6_R81.php

SMELL THE ROSES
AT THE BETTER HOMES & GARDENS TEST GARDEN®

If you have ever picked up a *Better Homes & Gardens* magazine, you may have wondered where some of the beautiful photos are taken. You can visit the location where they test new plants, try new garden trends, and capture photos for their publications and website in downtown Des Moines. Not many are aware it is open to the public on select days from May through September. The test garden includes 22 distinct gardens filled with color, greenery, and beauty. Some of the most notable of these gardens are the courtyard, rose garden, and clay garden. Take a seat and relax on one of the many benches and patio tables or take a stroll along the main path. You will want to make more than one visit throughout the year to capture different blooms each time.

1716 Locust St., 515-284-3994
bhg.com/gardening/design/test-garden-secrets

RUN, SKATE, AND PLAY
AT THE MIDAMERICAN
ENERGY COMPANY RECPLEX

This one-of-a-kind destination is well known as a hub for competition sports including hockey and youth sports programs, but the MidAmerican Energy Company RecPlex welcomes everyone of all abilities and has something to offer for all sports levels. The 300,000-square-foot complex offers fun activities for the public and holds conventions, concerts, community events, and more. Visitors can skate around on one of two public, indoor ice-skating rinks; play pickleball on one of three pickleball courts; play on the indoor turf during open play hours; or check out the ESports Arena, an area that contains water-cooled computers, six game consoles, and lounging. Iowa gets cold, and this facility offers year-round access to many sports and activities that would otherwise have to wait until the warmer months.

6500 Grand Ave., West Des Moines, 515-440-4820
therecplex.com

TIP
Take a look at the events calendar before going to know open play hours and other activities planned for the day.

"HIKE"
THROUGH THE DES MOINES SKYWALKS

The downtown Des Moines skywalk system is quite impressive . . . and incredibly beneficial in the frigid Iowa winters. The system is 4.2 miles in length and connects 55 buildings and 12 parking ramps. The climate-controlled skywalks enable you to get to places like hotels, restaurants, and coffee shops with ease. Park at one location and explore downtown Des Moines indoors through the skywalk system. You will find many walkers and families with young kids burning off energy on a cold Iowa day. The system links other places of interest as well, such as the Iowa Events Center, Wells Fargo Arena, and the Catch Des Moines Information Center. It can be easy to get lost! Make sure you have easy access to the interactive map before you go.

dsm.city/departments/engineering_-_division/skywalks.php

CHECK OUT
THE LEGENDARY PRINCIPAL CHARITY CLASSIC

The Principal Charity Classic brings PGA Tour Champions players together with central Iowa businesses and families to benefit Iowa children's charities. Breaking records and winning many awards over the years, the Principal Charity Classic is much more than a PGA Tour golf tournament. The annual golf outing held at Wakonda Club has raised millions of dollars since Principal took over as title sponsor in 2007. Iowans plan their work schedule around this charitable event. Each day of the event provides opportunities for golf, networking, and family fun. And whether you want to be involved as a volunteer or a spectator, there are chances to do so!

3915 Fleur Dr.
principalcharityclassic.com

SATISFY YOUR NEED FOR SPEED
AT THE IOWA SPEEDWAY

Located about 30 miles east of Des Moines, the Iowa Speedway in Newton has hosted the NASCAR Camping World Truck Series and Xfinity Series races since 2009. The high-speed track is the only track designed by a former driver, NASCAR Hall of Famer Rusty Wallace. The premier event of the track is the Hy-Vee IndyCar Race Weekend held every July. The entire weekend is filled with racing fun and concerts with big names such as Tim McGraw, Gwen Stefani, and others. Interested in becoming the next big race car driver? The Iowa Speedway provides opportunities to experience the speedway by driving a race car. The Rusty Wallace Racing Excellence and the Formula Experience are driving schools that bring these experiences to life. Bonus! Iowa Speedway is known for having a friendly atmosphere as crowds love the short-track action.

3333 Rusty Wallace Dr., Newton
iowaspeedway.com

Hall of Laureates

CULTURE
AND HISTORY

TAKE IN IOWA HISTORY
AT THE STATE HISTORICAL
MUSEUM OF IOWA

If you are looking to take in a bit of Iowa history, a visit to the State Historical Museum of Iowa is a must. This museum rich in history is located within the downtown State Historical Building of Iowa and offers three floors of exhibits and displays. Learn about the people and places that make Iowa what it is today, looking back as early as the American Indian settlements. Or look at real-life mammoth bones that were discovered on the floor of the Raccoon River Valley. One popular exhibit is Hollywood in the Heartland, where you can learn more about many classic movies that were filmed in Iowa, including *Field of Dreams* and *The Bridges of Madison County*. Entry into the museum is free, and it's a wonderful attraction for all ages.

600 E Locust St., 515-281-5111
iowaculture.gov/history/museum

TIP

If you have young children, make sure you stop in the Hands-On History room where children can take a closer look at a geode (the state rock of Iowa), create crayon rubbings, and play in the kitchen.

WANDER THROUGH LARGER-THAN-LIFE SCULPTURES
AT THE PAPPAJOHN SCULPTURE PARK

In downtown Des Moines, you will discover a 4.4-acre park filled with beautiful sculptures from some of the world's most famous artists. Grab lunch or dinner at one of the many restaurants surrounding the park and have a picnic or take a stroll around the walking path. Enjoy the unforgettable views of the downtown Des Moines skyline and take in the green landscape that makes Pappajohn Sculpture Park an extension of the Des Moines Art Center. Walk into the Nomade sculpture, a popular place for photos, or kiss a loved one in front of the LOVE sculpture. The panoramic awareness pavilion is a fun sculpture for kids to explore and another unique place to take colorful pictures. You can explore more than two dozen sculptures on your own or listen to an audio tour with your cell phone to learn about each piece.

1330 Grand Ave.
desmoinesartcenter.org/visit/pappajohn-sculpture-park

EXPERIENCE THE ARTS
AT THE ANNUAL DES MOINES ARTS FESTIVAL

The Des Moines Arts Festival has been located in several spots throughout Des Moines since its inception in 1958. Today, you can attend this three-day festival in downtown Des Moines at Western Gateway Park every June. Every year thousands attend this free festival that celebrates arts and culture. Beyond the expected paintings, photography, and other static visual arts, the festival also offers music, film, food, hands-on activities, and live entertainment. There is something for everyone to enjoy. Everyone is invited to support a local artist by purchasing art, creating their own art in the many activities offered throughout the weekend, or learning about different cultures and how they express themselves through art.

1205 Locust St., 515-416-6066
desmoinesartsfestival.org

TOUR A STOP ON THE UNDERGROUND RAILROAD
AT THE JORDAN HOUSE MUSEUM

In the early 1840s, famous abolitionist James C. Jordan settled in central Iowa. After falling in love with the land and area, his family began building their home, which today we refer to as the Jordan House Museum. During the antebellum period, the Jordan House was a designated spot on the Underground Railroad. The house also was a stop for travelers heading west. Many sought Jordan and his home due to his warm hospitality. In later years, Jordan played a huge role in central Iowa development by organizing the State Bank of Des Moines and serving in both the Iowa Senate and Iowa House of Representatives. Jordan also played a huge role in relocating the state capitol from Iowa City to Des Moines. Today, the house is a museum of West Des Moines history and holds many antiques and treasures, including a specific Underground Railroad Exhibit.

2001 Fuller Rd., West Des Moines, 515-225-1286
wdmhs.org/the-jordan-house

TAKE AN INSIDE LOOK
AT THE IOWA STATE CAPITOL

The Iowa State Capitol is, in a word, grand. If you're driving through downtown Des Moines, it is hard to miss the gold and shiny domes on the east side of the Des Moines River. The Iowa State Capitol is the only five-domed capitol in the United States. The century-old building features a 275-foot gold-leafed dome and four smaller domes, a marble grand staircase and woodwork, legislative and old supreme court chambers, governor's office, law library, and a scale model of the USS *Iowa* battleship. There is so much to see, and even more to learn. Thankfully, free guided tours are offered Monday through Saturday and can be scheduled by calling the Iowa Capitol Visitor Center. Throughout the tour, you'll hear a lot about the capitol, from its history to the interior decor to funny stories about our state senators. You can even go up into the famed dome and see it in all its splendor.

1007 E Grand Ave., 515-281-5591
legis.iowa.gov/resources/tourcapitol

LEARN ABOUT THE MIDWESTERN RURAL LIFE
AT LIVING HISTORY FARMS

You could spend a whole day at Living History Farms and still want more. That's how much fun it is exploring the 500-acre open-air museum located in Urbandale. Living History Farms educates and connects all people to the stories from many years ago. When you visit, you can explore the farms at your own pace. As you explore, you will travel through different historical periods that span 300 years. To make the experience even more unique, Living History Farms has on-site interpreters who are dressed according to their historical period and participate in activities and demonstrations. You will enjoy walking trails and riding on tractor-drawn carts that connect the 1876 Town of Walnut Hill to each of the historical farms. Living History Farms also hosts day camps, historic dinners, historic skills classes, and much more. And during the holiday season, Living History Farms lends itself to Santa's Rock n Lights, a drive-through light show. It's truly an experience!

11121 Hickman Rd., Urbandale, 515-278-5286
lhf.org

TOUR THE HOME
OF MR. AND MRS. IOWA
AT TERRACE HILL

Terrace Hill is the Iowa governor's residence and a National Historic Landmark. Completed in 1869, the residence has intrigued and inspired since the first guests walked through its doors for the housewarming party of Arathusa and Benjamin Franklin Allen on January 29, 1869. The first governor to live in Terrace Hill was Governor Robert Ray, who moved into the 18,000-square-foot residence with his family in 1976. Today, you can experience Terrace Hill's history and stunning architecture firsthand during an hour-long guided tour, offered March through December. During it, you can expect to see the carriage house, the first and second floors of the residence, and the historic gardens.

2300 Grand Ave., 515-281-7205
terracehill.iowa.gov

TIP

Terrace Hill hosts nearly 10,000 visitors each year, from buses of schoolchildren to political figures and foreign diplomats.

TOUR A "NATIONAL TREASURE,"
THE 1920S SALISBURY HOUSE

Salisbury House draws thousands of visitors each year . . . and for good reason. It's a true landmark. The house's extensive grounds, gorgeous architecture, and world-class collections offer an experience unlike any other. The Salisbury House was built in the 1920s by cosmetics magnate Carl Weeks and his wife, Edith, and contains authentic 16th-century English oak woodwork, English flintwork, and rafters that date back to the time of Shakespeare. Today, you can visit the Salisbury House and take either a self-guided or guided tour of the home. You'll enjoy seeing the family's original collection of artworks, tapestries, antique furnishings, and much more. There are also a number of public events and programs held at the Salisbury House throughout the year, like the spring fundraising garden party, afternoon tea at Tea at the Castle, and the popular Holly and Ivy holiday home tour fundraiser.

4025 Tonawanda Dr., 515-274-1777
salisburyhouse.org

CELEBRATE FOOD AND MUSIC ACROSS THE WORLD
AT THE WORLD FOOD & MUSIC FESTIVAL

What could possibly be better than a festival dedicated to all things food and music? The annual World Food & Music Festival, held in downtown Des Moines, offers international cuisine, live music and performing arts, cooking demonstrations, interactive programs, wine, craft beers, and much more. One especially exciting aspect of the festival to witness are the cooking challenges. For music, you can expect to hear everything from Spanish salsa music to the soaring vocals of Celtic folk songs. And for food, you'll have so many options from around the globe that it'll be hard to narrow down what to fill your tummy up with. In fact, at 2022's festival, about 50 food vendors representing 27 countries set up shop. One thing is for sure if you're attending the World Food & Music Festival . . . show up hungry!

1330 Grand Ave.
dsmpartnership.com/worldfoodandmusicfestival

SUPPORT
LOCAL ARTISTS
AT MAINFRAME STUDIOS

Mainframe Studios is a Des Moines nonprofit providing permanent, affordable workspaces for artists of all disciplines. It's also the largest nonprofit arts studio in the nation. In total, Mainframe Studios offers 180 different creative workspaces over a total of five floors. This is a great place to visit to learn or participate in new arts such as handblown stained-glass art, painting, dance, music, photography, and much more. The space also hosts events of all kinds for the public to enjoy, like youth and adult art classes and First Friday. This event happens on the first Friday of every month and is your chance to tour the artists' studios, enjoy special exhibitions, eat food, and listen to live music. Bonus! First Friday is always free and open to the public.

900 Keosauqua Way, 515-216-4253
mainframestudios.org

TAKE A TOUR
OF DES MOINES'S MURALS

Des Moines boasts some incredible murals. Discovering some of these pieces of public art is a fun outdoor activity you can get your whole family behind. Downtown, you'll find murals including *Cheers from Des Moines* by Ben Schuh on the side of Exile Brewing Company. Also Instagram-worthy is *My Heart Belongs to Des Moines* by Jenna Brownlee. You'll also find whimsical pieces in Beaverdale, at the Outlets of Des Moines in Altoona, and at West Des Moines's West Glen Town Center. There are also a few murals throughout the District in Ankeny that you may have seen pop up on your social media before. There's a reason why Des Moines is a celebrated arts destination in the Midwest, so get out there and explore! You can also make your tour around town easier by downloading the Greater Des Moines Public Art Foundation app.

LEARN ABOUT WORLD HUNGER
AT THE WORLD FOOD PRIZE HALL OF LAUREATES

The Dr. Norman E. Borlaug World Food Prize Hall of Laureates is a true Des Moines gem. The Hall of Laureates is located within the restored, century-old Des Moines Public Library Building that's now home to the World Food Prize. The building serves as a number of things, including a museum recognizing the great achievements in agriculture and fighting hunger, a convocation center to hold events during the World Food Prize International Symposium, and an educational facility featuring interactive displays on hunger and food security. You can visit the Hall of Laureates yourself on a public or private tour. You can also take a stroll anytime through the outdoor garden, which is a key feature of the Principal Riverwalk. And if it's the holiday season, be sure to attend the free World Food Prize Hall of Laureates Holiday Open House.

100 Locust St., 515-245-3735
halloflaureates.org

TAKE A WHIRL
ON THE UNION PARK
HERITAGE CAROUSEL

Did you know Des Moines has its own carousel? It's true! Located in historic Union Park, the hand-carved, hand-painted gem with 30 whimsical animals and two chariots is the first wood carousel built since the 1930s. On the walls of the carousel are hand-painted murals depicting the heritage of Des Moines as well. Children can take a ride on the carousel for just 50 cents, and adults for just one dollar. The Heritage Carousel is also available for rent for private events like birthday parties, family reunions, and company outings. Rentals include rides, music from the band organ, and picnic tables. How fun! And after your ride on the carousel, you can enjoy Union Park itself, one of Des Moines's oldest parks, and its rocket slide, wading pool, floral garden, and more.

1801 Pennsylvania Ave., 515-323-8200
heritagecarousel.org

TAKE A RIDE
ON THE BOONE & SCENIC VALLEY RAILROAD

The Boone & Scenic Valley Railroad is a museum unlike any other. Not only will you learn about the history of railroading in Iowa on your visit, you can also hop aboard a train and experience it for yourself! There are numerous different train rides available, like a Dinner Train and the Picnic Train, which is especially popular with families and enables you to bring your own lunch. You can also enjoy a fun trip aboard the Fraser Excursion train or a relaxing Valentine's dinner train ride. New to the Boone & Scenic Valley Railroad is its Rail Explorers attraction. During a 12.5-mile round-trip, open-air tour, visitors zip along the tracks on a motor-powered rail bike. You'll also cross the 156-foot-high Bass Point Creek High Trestle Bridge and take in panoramic views of the Des Moines River Valley. After your railroad adventure, be sure to stop by and see the Kate Shelley High Bridge, one of the highest and longest double-track railroad bridges in the United States.

225 10th St., Boone, 515-432-4249
bsvrr.com/wp

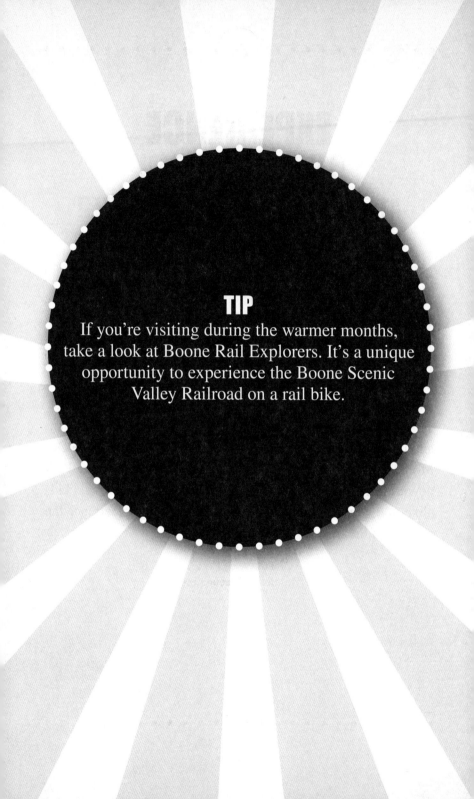

TIP

If you're visiting during the warmer months, take a look at Boone Rail Explorers. It's a unique opportunity to experience the Boone Scenic Valley Railroad on a rail bike.

EXPERIENCE ART UP CLOSE
AT THE DES MOINES ART CENTER

The Des Moines Art Center has an extraordinary collection of modern and contemporary art, as well as exciting exhibitions and educational programming. They pride themselves on providing opportunities for transformational art experiences for all. On your visit to the art center, admission is free. You'll witness an impressive collection of art from the 19th century to the present, including major works by Edward Hopper, Georgia O'Keeffe, and Francis Bacon. You can take a guided or self-guided tour; shop the art center's extensive collection of books, jewelry, and more; and enjoy a meal at the museum restaurant. The Des Moines Art Center also oversees the Pappajohn Sculpture Park downtown. They host a number of art classes for adults and kids alike, too. Ultimately, there are so many ways to experience the wonder of the Des Moines Art Center!

4700 Grand Ave., 515-277-4405
desmoinesartcenter.org

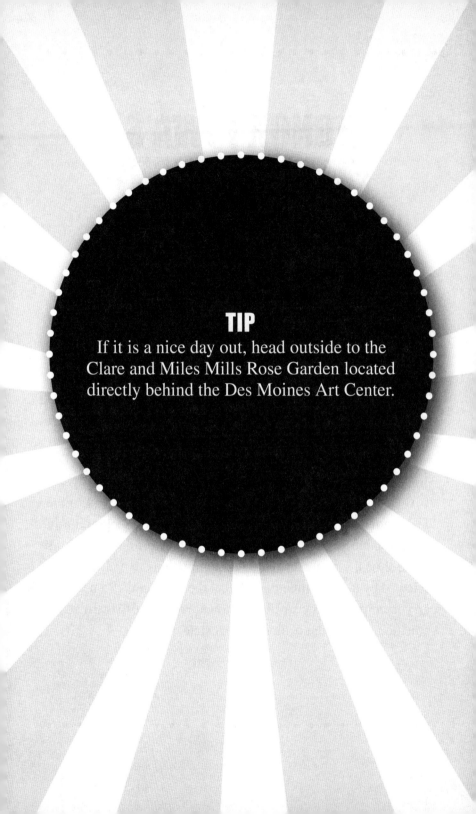

TIP

If it is a nice day out, head outside to the Clare and Miles Mills Rose Garden located directly behind the Des Moines Art Center.

HONOR IOWA'S EXTRAORDINARY WOMEN
AT THE IOWA WOMEN OF ACHIEVEMENT BRIDGE

If you've ever been downtown enjoying all it has to offer, there's a chance you've crossed the Iowa Women of Achievement Bridge, which links the east and west sides of Des Moines at the northern edge of the Principal Riverwalk loop. The bridge features one pathway for joggers and walkers, and another for cyclists. At night, it's lit up by colorful lights that reflect on the water and make for a photo-worthy moment. The city of Des Moines installed the Iowa Women of Achievement Bridge in 2010 to celebrate historical Iowa women's contributions to the local, national, and global community. Each year beginning in 2013, notable women from Iowa's history are honored at this bridge. Local citizens provide the nominations, which are then reviewed by a committee that selects the recipients. So not only can you enjoy a scenic stroll downtown, you can also learn about some notable women from our great state.

Principal Riverwalk

LEARN ABOUT IOWA VETERANS
AT THE IOWA GOLD STAR
MILITARY MUSEUM

Located within Camp Dodge in Johnston, the Iowa Gold Star Military Museum honors the heroic service of all Iowa veterans. There are a number of exhibits within the museum, including ones focused on every war since the Spanish–American War. Each one highlights materials that tell the story of Iowa's military past. On your free visit, you'll walk through the museum filled with artifacts, as well as have the opportunity to stop by the reference library on military subjects and Iowa veterans. One highlight is the Civil War exhibit, which features a full-sized diorama depicting Iowa troops at the April 1862 Battle of Shiloh, and an interactive "wheel of fate" utilizing Civil War casualty and service statistics for Iowa volunteers that tempts visitors to determine their chances of survival with the push of a button. Visiting the Iowa Gold Star Military Museum is a wonderful way to learn about our past while honoring those who've served.

7105 NW 70th Ave., Johnston, 515-252-4531
goldstarmuseum.iowa.gov

CELEBRATE DIVERSITY
AT THE ROBERT D. RAY ASIAN GARDENS

What draws the eye to the Robert D. Ray Asian Gardens downtown is the beautiful, vibrant red, 37-foot-tall Asian pavilion along the Principal Riverwalk. But there's so much more to the gardens to explore. The gardens sit on 1.7 acres along the Des Moines River and are a symbol of diversity and appreciation for the contribution of Asian Americans in Iowa. They also recognize the lasting impact of Governor Robert D. Ray, who led the way in Des Moines being the first city in the US to accept Vietnamese refugees. The area features Asian sculptures and lanterns, as well as a Character Garden with six granite boulders. After strolling through the tranquil gardens, you can continue along the Principal Riverwalk, which connects to a number of other downtown spots.

Robert D. Ray Dr.

SEE LOCAL GOVERNMENT IN ACTION
AT THE JUDICIAL BRANCH BUILDING

The Iowa Judicial Branch Building is easily recognizable by its blue dome. The building houses the Iowa Supreme Court, the Iowa Court of Appeals, and state court administration. You can take a self-guided tour of the five-story limestone building, where you'll find historic allegorical murals from the 1880s, marble floors, and stately courtrooms. The Judicial Branch Building is open to the public for visits weekdays from 8 a.m. to 4:30 p.m. When oral arguments for the supreme court and court of appeals are heard, the public is welcome to attend and watch as well. Group tours for more than 20 can be scheduled ahead of your arrival, or a self-guided tour sheet is available for individuals. What a great way to experience our local government in action and learn about its history firsthand.

1111 E Court Ave.
iowacourts.gov/for-the-public/educational-resources-and-services/
judicial-branch-building-and-courthouse-tours

CHERISH THE PAST
AT SURETY HOTEL

The Surety Hotel preserves Des Moines's past while offering a four-star stay and unique experience for guests. The former Iowa Loan & Trust Co. building is a one-of-a-kind gem and has been restored to highlight its original elements. Built in 1913, the Midland Building—the Surety Hotel's former name—was the tallest building in the state. Now it's not, of course, but the Surety Hotel makes a point to uphold its connection to local makers and creatives by doing things like serving guests food on hand-thrown ceramics and providing local coffee. The building also houses Mulberry Street Tavern and Surety Courtyard, a private space that serves drinks, light bites, and occasional live music during the summer months. It's a popular spot to rent for personal and professional events like weddings, meetings, family reunions, and more.

206 6th Ave., 515-985-2066
suretyhotel.com

CONNECT WITH ART, MUSIC, AND HISTORY
AT HOYT SHERMAN PLACE

Hoyt Sherman Place is a beautiful mansion located in Sherman Hill, one of Des Moines's most historic areas. The venue offers an intimate theater experience, as well as a captivating art gallery. Hoyt Sherman Place is the former family home of Hoyt Sherman, built in 1877. Today, it serves as a cultural destination where people can connect with art, music, and history. People can rent out the theater, art gallery, or the Center for Artists and Education for any number of events. There's also the Barry Bauman Art Institute, which offers arts programming for children and adults and honors the generosity of the Chicago-based art conservator who donated over a million dollars in free restoration services to Hoyt Sherman Place. Or, perhaps you want to tour the Hoyt Sherman mansion or attend a concert. You can do all this and more at Hoyt Sherman Place!

1501 Woodland Ave., 515-244-0507
hoytsherman.org

Storyhouse Bookpub

SHOPPING
AND FASHION

DISCOVER A TREASURE
AT WEST END ARCHITECTURAL
SALVAGE

Go on a treasure hunt! Whether you love to search for hidden gems and antiques or just to walk down memory lane, West End Architectural Salvage is a shopping experience for all ages. Before you start to wander through four floors of someone else's junk, stop at their coffee shop for a warm latte. You can also enjoy a glass of wine, local beer, or a cocktail. Their team of pickers and artists travel all over the world looking for one-of-a-kind furniture or items to reclaim. While walking through, you will likely come across something that will bring you back to your childhood or discover the one piece that has been missing from your home. There is not one bare spot in the entire store. You will surely leave feeling inspired and want to return.

22 9th St., 515-243-4405
westendsalvage.com

SUPPORT LOCAL FARMERS AND MAKERS
AT THE DOWNTOWN DES MOINES FARMERS' MARKET

Nothing beats farm-fresh produce and handmade items. The Downtown Des Moines Farmers' Market is located in downtown Des Moines on Court Avenue in front of the Polk County Courthouse. It spans a few blocks toward the Des Moines Riverwalk. Since 1975, every Saturday morning between May and October, the city of Des Moines wakes up and makes its way down to one of the most popular farmers markets in the Midwest according to *Midwest Living* magazine. It's a summer tradition to eat breakfast, meet friends, listen to live music, participate in various activities each week, and shop for weekly groceries or a gift for a loved one. Kids enjoy the farmers market too! They can hop on a small train, find a balloon artist, or get their face painted. A fun outing for the entire family.

300 Court Ave.
dsmpartnership.com/desmoinesfarmersmarket

TIP
Each year the Downtown Des Moines Farmers' Market also offers a winter market, which happens twice during the winter and holiday season.

SHOP ONE OF THE MOST DIVERSE DISTRICTS
IN DES MOINES: THE EAST VILLAGE

There are more than 100 local shops and eats to experience in the East Village, so it's hard to know where to start your day of shopping. The area features historic buildings, boutique retail spots, and award-winning restaurants, making it one of the trendiest neighborhoods around. The East Village begins at the Des Moines River and extends east to the Iowa State Capitol building. Some highlights of the area include Raygun, a clothing company owned and operated by "extremely attractive Midwesterners"; a rooftop bar called the Republic on Grand; and Up-Down Arcade Bar, which features more than 40 arcade games from the '80s and '90s. The whole family will get a kick out of the annual Historic East Village Holiday Promenade, which is held each November and is a festive celebration that includes fireworks, carolers, horse-drawn carriage rides, and more.

Downtown Des Moines between
the Des Moines River and the Iowa State Capitol
eastvillagedesmoines.com

STOP BY
THE HISTORIC VALLEY JUNCTION

Valley Junction has a storied history. The area is the foundation of West Des Moines. Long before it became the vibrant and fun shopping district that it is today, Valley Junction was founded by a cattle rancher from Virginia named James Cunningham Jordan. The area gained its name from the importance railroads played in forming the town. It was a hub for many different railway companies and officially became a city in 1893. Today, you can explore Valley Junction and its many shops and restaurants, including Heart of Iowa Marketplace, Rose's Theatrical Supply, Cooper's on 5th, and the Hall DSM. You could easily spend a whole day in the area, soaking up all the unique offerings Valley Junction has to provide while supporting local.

5th and side streets in West Des Moines
valleyjunction.com

SHOP
AT THE JORDAN CREEK TOWN CENTER

Jordan Creek Town Center attracts visitors from far and wide because of its expansive shopping options. In fact, it's the largest shopping complex in Iowa. The mall itself is filled with a collection of brand-name stores and some quick-and-easy eating spots as well. They also have a 20-screen movie theater and a parklike atmosphere with a lakefront boardwalk that offers an amphitheater with live music during the summer months. The mall continues to add new stores and has nearby entertainment options like Smash Park and Spare Time, which features bowling lanes, an arcade, and laser tag. The area also offers hotels nearby, making it easy for visitors to plan a whole day or weekend enjoying all that Jordan Creek Town Center has to offer.

101 Jordan Creek Pkwy., West Des Moines, 515-224-5000
jordancreektowncenter.com/en.html

SAVE SOME MONEY
AT THE OUTLETS OF DES MOINES

Outlets of Des Moines brings a number of brand names to the Altoona shopping destination. The open-air outlet mall is the only of its kind in the Des Moines metro and is conveniently located at the intersection of Interstate 80 and US-65. Being an outlet mall, you can save a good chunk of money at your favorite stores like Under Armour, Old Navy, Michael Kors, and so many others. After a few hours of shopping at the 50-plus outlet stores, you can refuel with food from places like Auntie Anne's or Charleys Philly Steaks. Keep an eye out for different events throughout the year, too, like the Midwest Vendor Market.

801 Bass Pro Dr. NW, Altoona, 515-380-7400
outletsofdesmoines.com

GET YOUR READ ON
AT LOCAL BOOKSTORES

Book lovers, rejoice! Des Moines boasts a number of locally owned bookstores. Take, for instance, Beaverdale Books, which has served the Beaverdale neighborhood since 2006. They also host a number of author events throughout the year, which are fun to attend. More recent to the Historic East Village is Storyhouse Bookpub, which actually got its start out of the owner's garage during the COVID-19 pandemic. It, too, puts on a number of events, like author visits and children's story times. Also in the East Village is Plain Talk Books, which sells a curated selection of used books in a cozy café setting. And new to Valley Junction is Reading in Public. The store does fun things as well, like hosting a variety of genre-based book clubs. In Ankeny, stop by Walls of Books, where you can even earn store credit for bringing in your old reads.

Beaverdale Books
2629 Beaver Ave., 515-279-5400
beaverdalebooks.com

Storyhouse Bookpub
505 E Grand Ave., Ste. 102
storyhousebookpub.com

Plain Talk Books & Coffee
602 E Grand Ave., 515-243-0815
raccoonforks.com/plaintalk

Reading in Public Bookstore & Cafe
315 5th St., Ste. 100, West Des Moines, 515-864-9089
readinginpublic.com

Walls of Books
613 N Ankeny Blvd., Ankeny, 515-381-0017
wallsofbooks.net

SHOP 'TIL YOU DROP
IN THE DISTRICT AT PRAIRIE TRAIL

If you're in Ankeny, be sure to make a visit to the District at Prairie Trail. This entertainment center in the middle of town is a go-to spot for shopping, drinks, and yummy food from local restaurants like Fong's Pizza and District 36 Wine Bar & Grille. The growing area puts on a number of events throughout the year, including Dazzling in the District, Pizza Fest, and Sips and Songs. For some extra family fun, there's also B&B Theatre Ankeny 12 and B-Roll Bowling, as well the Operating Room, a bar arcade. The Ankeny Kirkendall Public Library is located in the center, too, and offers tons of resources and events for all ages. The District seems to continually add new options, so you can be sure to find something fun to do no matter when you visit!

SW District Dr., Ankeny
thedistrictpt.com

SUPPORT HISTORIC
OAK PARK AND HIGHLAND PARK
NEIGHBORHOOD

In the early 1920s, the Oak Park and Highland Park neighborhood was a busy business district in Des Moines. Also referred to as the "streetcar suburb," it was a popular place for residents to work and live due to the location of downtown Des Moines. Over the years, this area of Des Moines was forgotten, but in recent years it has received much love and attention. Today, it is listed on the National Register of Historic Places. It now offers many great places to shop and eat. Grab a coffee from the Slow Down Coffee Co. or a sweet treat from the Highland Bakery. Shop for local home goods, soaps, books, sustainable items, and more at the Des Moines Mercantile or the Collective. If you are a plant lover, you will want to walk through the Art Terrarium, which is a plant oasis. As you walk through the neighborhood, take a moment to stop and look at the murals and grab dinner at Chuck's Restaurant.

Euclid and 6th Avenues
highlandoakdsm.wordpress.com

Adventureland Amusement Park

ACTIVITIES
BY SEASON

SPRING

Learn More about the Wild at Water Works Park, 79

Watch a Future Olympian Compete at the Drake Relays, 75

Enjoy All Things Outdoors at Jester Park, 54

Experience Art Up Close at the Des Moines Art Center, 110

Enjoy the Outdoors, Indoors at the Greater Des Moines Botanical Garden, 60

SUMMER

Take a Thrill Ride at Adventureland Amusement Park, 58

Enjoy the Outdoors at Jasper Winery, 34

Rock Out to Diverse Music at 80/35 Music Festival, 45

Support Local Farmers and Makers at the Downtown Des Moines Farmers' Market, 121

Check Out the Legendary Principal Charity Classic, 90

View the Painted Sky during the National Balloon Classic, 67

Enjoy the Best Days Ever at the Iowa State Fair, 62

• •

FALL

WINTER

Howell's Pumpkins

Science Center of Iowa

SUGGESTED
ITINERARIES

DATE NIGHT

Enjoy World-Class Entertainment and Culture
 with Des Moines Performing Arts, 38

Enjoy a Specialty Cocktail at a Cocktail Bar, 12

Try a Midwest Steak Dish Specialty, 6

Experience Upscale Dining at 801 Chophouse, 28

Take a Sip of Fresh, Crisp Apples at Winterset Cidery, 23

Listen to a Live Jazz Show at Noce, 42

Sip on an Iowa Beer at the Iowa Taproom, 5

FAMILY DAY WITH THE KIDS

Make Zoo Friends at the Blank Park Zoo, 63

Use Your Imagination and Play at the Des Moines
 Children's Museum, 69

Support the Community's Rising Stars at the
 Des Moines Playhouse, 39

Become a Future Scientist at the Science Center of Iowa, 68

STEP BACK IN HISTORY

Historic East Village

Lauridsen Skatepark

INDEX

• •

• •

• •

• •